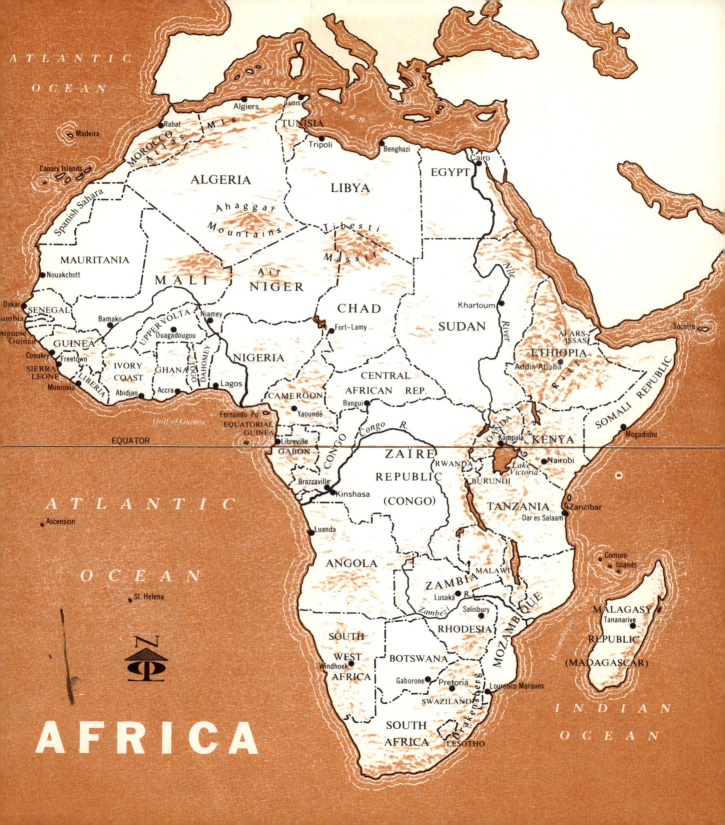

Enchantment of Africa

MALI

by ALLAN CARPENTER,
THOMAS O'TOOLE, AND MARK LA POINTE

Consulting Editor
Charles Berberich
Department of History
Northwestern University
Evanston, Illinois

 CHILDRENS PRESS, CHICAGO

THE ENCHANTMENT OF AFRICA

Available now: Botswana, Burundi, Egypt, Kenya, Lesotho, Liberia, Mali, Malagasy Republic (Madagascar), Rhodesia, Rwanda, Sierra Leone, Swaziland, Tanzania, Tunisia, Uganda, Upper Volta, Zaïre Republic (Congo Kinshasa), Zambia

Planned for the future: Algeria, Cameroon, Central African Republic, Chad, Congo (Brazzaville), Dahomey, Equatorial Guinea, Ethiopia, Gambia, Gabon, Ghana, Guinea, Ivory Coast, Libya, Malawi, Mauritania, Morocco, Niger, Nigeria, Senegal, Somali Republic, South Africa, Sudan, Togo

ACKNOWLEDGMENTS

John D. Garner, Public Affairs Officer, United States Information Service, Bamako, Mali; L'Office Malien de Touriseme, Bamako, Mali; Societe Hotelleries du Mali, Bamako, Mali; Ministry of Health, Bamako, Mali.

Cover Photograph: Prehistoric Dogon cave paintings, Mark LaPointe
Frontispiece: Dogon village chieftain at Dogon village of Irely on the slopes of Sanga Cliff, United Nations

Project Editor: Joan Downing
Manuscript Editor: Janis Fortman
Map Artist: Donald G. Bouma

LIBRARY OF CONGRESS
CATALOGING IN PUBLICATION DATA

Carpenter, John Allan, 1917-
  Mali.
  (Enchantment of Africa)
  SUMMARY: An introduction to the geography, people, history, government, resources, culture, and major cities of Mali.
  1. Mali—Juvenile literature. [1. Mali] I. O'Toole, Thomas, 1941- joint author. II. LaPointe, Mark, joint author. III. Title.
DT551.C37   966'.23   75-2269
ISBN 0-516-04574-1

Contents

A True Story to Set the Scene

In 1325 the Songhai Empire was declining. Two young princes, Ali Kolon and Salman Nar, lived a happy and contented life in Gao, the capital of the Songhai Empire and a bustling city of trade. Their father, Dia Assibai, seemed to them to be the most powerful man in the world. Because they were Muslims (followers of the Islam religion), each day Ali and Salman went to the mosque, where they were taught to read and write Arabic.

One spring morning, as Moroccan and Tunisian merchants swarmed through the streets of Gao, a great army appeared on the plains outside the city: infantry armed with spears, archers with quivers full of arrows, and cavalry troops mounted on camels and horses. Soon the soldiers of Mali had occupied Gao and had captured Ali and Salman.

Fortunately for the boys, Mansa Musa (the emperor of Mali) was returning from his pilgrimage to Mecca (the Muslim holy city); he came to Gao to take control of the city. As was the custom, Mansa Musa took the emperor's sons, Ali and Salman, with him to his own capital of Niani. The two boys, torn from their home, were held captive by Mansa Musa to ensure that their father would not revolt against the taxes imposed on him by the Mali Empire.

Eventually the boys grew to accept their lot; they became caught up in the daily life of the powerful Mali Empire. But the boys

Opposite: This boy reading the Koran *is learning Arabic in the same way Ali Kolon and Salman Nar did in the fourteenth century.*

never forgot their homeland or that they were princes of the Songhai Empire. Together they learned all they could about Mali. As pages in the king's court at Niani, they learned royal etiquette. Because the power and wealth of Mali attracted teachers from far and wide, the boys were able to continue their education in Arabic. Along with the sons of other rulers in Mali, Ali and Salman were trained as soldiers. The two brothers learned their lessons well, but secretly they remained loyal to Gao.

As the boys grew older, they became excellent soldiers. Ali especially showed ability as a fighter and leader, so Mansa Musa gave him a position in Mali's army.

By the time Mansa Musa died in 1332, both Ali and Salman had become military officers. In this capacity, Ali and Salman were able to learn the strengths and weaknesses of the Mali Empire. They built up a number of troops that were loyal to them and came to know the empire's trade routes and military posts. But no one in the busy court noticed that each military expedition that Ali Kolon and Salman Nar led took them closer to their home in Gao. Nor did the court know that these young officers were hiding spears and grain along a route to Gao.

Mansa Musa's death set off a struggle for succession between his son and his brother. Ali and Salman wasted little time: they gathered a number of the loyal troops and left on horseback for Gao.

On arriving in their native city, Ali and Salman drove out the "puppet kings" who had replaced their father. Then they declared the Songhai Empire once again independent from Mali.

For the next century, the descendants of Ali Kolon continued to live in a restless sort of peace with the Mali Empire. The Songhai Empire was also constantly forced to fight against Tuareg raiders from the desert and Mossi cavalry from the south, who also wanted the riches of Gao. But because of the military training that Ali and Salman had received as boys in Mali, the Songhai Empire was able to defend its land successfully. The empire lasted until 1591, when it was invaded by a Moroccan army with firearms.

The Face of the Land

Mali is a large, landlocked country in the middle of French West Africa — very roughly shaped like the figure "8." With an area of 464,000 square miles, Mali is about the size of Texas, Oklahoma, and New Mexico combined. Mali is bordered by seven countries: Mauritania, Algeria, Niger, Upper Volta, Ivory Coast, Guinea, and Senegal.

Much of Mali is a vast plain, or *sahel*,

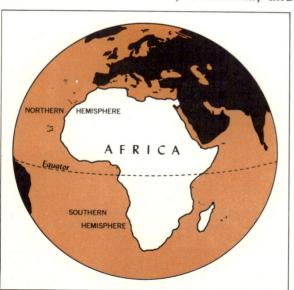

in the upper basins of the Senegal and Niger rivers. Western Mali is generally savanna land, with rolling hills and spectacular waterfalls on the many rivers. The Maninka Plateau rises in the southwest, meeting the highlands in neighboring Guinea. In the middle of the country is the marshy delta of the Niger River. This is an area of many rivers and lakes, including Lake Débo and Lake Faguibine. To the north, the grasslands thin out to desert. Mali extends far into the dry, dusty Sahara.

The climate varies greatly in different parts of the country. In the Sahara, rainfall averages less than one inch a year. The sahel is wetter, with about thirty-nine inches of rain a year. Rainfall is heaviest in the far south at Sikasso, where an average of fifty-nine inches of rain fall each year.

A GREAT RIVER

Cutting diagonally across the southern two thirds of the country is the Niger River, the third-largest river in Africa. The Niger River rises in Guinea and flows more than six hundred miles northeast, then turns east at Timbuktu and flows south toward the Atlantic Ocean. By the time it reaches the Atlantic in south-central Nigeria, the Niger River has traveled twenty-six hundred miles.

In the center of Mali are the great flood plains of the inland Niger delta. Here the Niger is joined by Bani, which flows north from the Ivory Coast. During the rainy season (May to October), these two rivers swell to overflowing, creating a maze of seasonal rivers, lakes, and swamps that last well into the dry season (October through April). Fishermen, farmers, and herdsmen

MAP KEY

Adrar des Iforas (Mountains), C-6	Bir Ounâne, C-4	Irely, E-4	Manankoro, G-2	Sanga, E-4
Almoustarat, D-5	Boré, E-4	Jenne, E-3	Markala, F-3	Saratere, E-4
Anefis, D-5	Borenta, E-4	Kabara, D-4	Mopti, E-3	Ségou, F-3
Ansongo, E-5	Bougoumi, F-2	Kadiolo, G-3	Mount Ilebjane, D-5	Senegal River, E-1
Araouane, C-4	Bourem, D-5	Kangaba, F-2	Mourdiah, E-2	Sikasso, F-3
Badalabougou, F-2	Dia, E-4	Kanioume, E-4	M'Pesoba, F-3	Sikasso Plateau, G-2
Badougou, G-2	Djikoroni, E-3	Karou, E-5	Nampala, E-3	Talak, D-6
Bafoulabé, F-1	Doro, D-5	Kati, F-2	Nara, E-2	Taoudeni, B-4
Bamako, F-2	Dossau, E-4	Kayes, E-1	Niafounke, E-3	Tazadite, A-3
Bamba, D-4	Douentza, E-4	Kidal, D-6	Niger River, D-5, F-2	Tebezas, D-6
Banamba, F-2	El Mzereb, A-3	Kita, F-1	Niono, E-3	Telatai, D-6
Bandiagara, E-4	Foum el Alba	Koulikoro, F-2	Nior edauu uahhel, E-1	Tenenkou, E-3
Bandiagara Cliffs, E-4	(Pass), C-4	Kouroukale, F-1	Nokara, E-4	Terhazza, B-3
Bani River, F-3	Ft. Pierre Bordes, C-6	Kourouninkoto, F-1	Ouelessebougou, F-2	Tessalit, C-5
Baoulé National Park, F-2	Gao, D-5	Koussane, E-1	Oyako Falls, F-1	Timbuktu, D-4
Baoulé River, F-2	Goundam, D-4	Koutiala, F-3	Sahara Desert, B-3, B-4	Timétrine, C-5
Bir el Ksaib, C-3	Gourma-Rharous, D-4	Lake Débo, E-3	Samanko, F-2	Wadi de l'Azaouak, D-6
	Hamdullahi, F-1	Lake Faguibine, D-3	San, F-3	Wadi du Tilemsi, D-5
		Lake Horo, E-3		Yoro, E-4

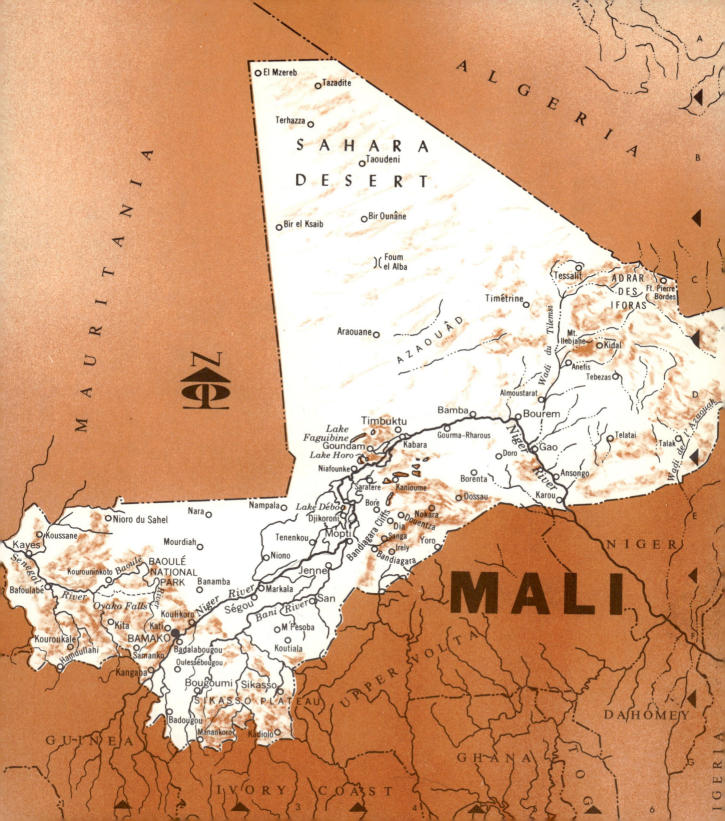

have all learned to profit from the abundant water in this rich valley, an oasis in an otherwise dry land.

To the east of the river valleys are the Kaarta Plateau and the Bandiagara Cliffs. The Maninka Plateau rises in the southwest, meeting the highlands in neighboring Guinea.

THE SPECTER OF DROUGHT

Mali has often faced periods of great drought. From late October to April, there is little rain in the country. Outside of the small areas along the rivers that can be irrigated, 90 percent of Mali's population — farmers and herders — depend on the yearly rains.

In 1968 rainfall was especially light; this was also the case in 1969, and in the next three years as well. By 1973 drought conditions prevailed. When the rains were late again in 1973, thousands of cattle and hundreds of people faced hunger and death from sickness in their weakened condition. But Mali was not the only drought-stricken African nation; five neighboring countries were in the same position. To help relieve the drought, massive amounts of grain and medical help were sent from the United States, China, and many European countries.

Unfortunately, the country's underlying problems continue. Marginally useful land has been pressed into production as the population has grown. Herds, watered by a few overworked wells, have been allowed to expand beyond the abilities of pastures to support them in dry years. Irrigation projects have not been fully used. Much farmable land in the Niger Delta is in the hands of the Fulbé, an old ruling group of landowners, who keep it for their herds.

And the threat of drought is always present. The growth of the desert that began ten thousand years ago continues. Perhaps man may someday control the climate, reforest the desert fringe, and irrigate large areas of the desert. But until then, it is necessary to control the herds, make full use of the irrigation now available, and attempt to improve production.

The third-largest river in Africa, the Niger cuts diagonally across the southern two thirds of Mali. The port of Mopti on the Niger (opposite) is a center of riverboat traffic.

13

Three Boys and Girls of Mali

AMADOU OF SANGA

Amadou lives with his family in Sanga, a village on the Bandiagara Cliffs. His people, the Dogon, are mostly farmers. They build their homes in limestone cliffs, as they have done for centuries. In this dry part of the country, the water trapped in hollows in the limestone is very important to the Dogon.

In the nearby valley are fields where millet is grown, harvested, and stored in granaries for the dry season. Almost everyone in the village works in the fields. Many people also grow onions, which they sell or trade for fish, meat, and sugar in nearby markets or at the town of Mopti on the Niger River.

Thirteen-year-old Amadou does not go to the fields very often. When he is not at

Opposite: Dogon cliff dwellings and granaries in the Bandiagara Cliffs. Amadou lives in the village of Sanga.

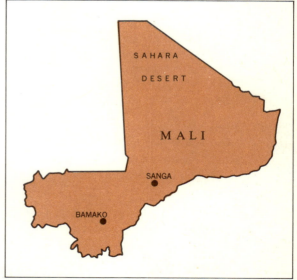

the village school, he can usually be found at his father's shop, learning his father's skills. Amadou's father is a blacksmith. Because iron hoes and tools are precious to these farming people, the man who can make them from iron ore or even old scrap iron is considered special — almost a magician. Thus, the Dogon highly respected the skills of blacksmiths.

Besides making tools and iron hoes, Amadou's father also makes the tools for wood carving. He is in charge of carving masks and making metal sculpture for the village's religious ceremonies. Amadou has watched his father make some of the common figures, but the masks for the ritual dances and sculpture of the dead are always done in secret.

This year Amadou was initiated into the Dogon society and acknowledged as an adult. He and the other boys of Sanga and the nearby village came as scheduled before the Hogon, or village priest. In many weeks of concentrated teaching, the Hogon and his helpers taught the boys Dogon secrets, beliefs, and history. By repainting ancient cave paintings and listening to their elders, Amadou and the other boys learned much about who they were as young men of the Dogon.

But Amadou has also been influenced by his uncle, Youssef, who is twenty-five and married. Youssef has just returned from a missionary school in the town of Bandiagara, about twenty miles from Sanga. At the missionary school, Youssef learned to read and write French and learned first-aid techniques. He was also converted to Christianity. Youssef thinks that Amadou should be baptized and go to this school in order to prepare himself for a place in the modern, changing world.

Until Youssef returned to the village, Amadou was certain that he would become a blacksmith like his father and carry on the ancient ways of his people. Now Amadou is not so certain. He loves and respects his father. The beautiful objects his father makes, the respect the people have for his father, and the things he has learned about the myths and beauties of Dogon teachings all attract him. But Youssef feels that knowledge is also important. When someone is hurt, needs to have a letter written, or has a problem with his onion crops, he comes to Youssef. Youssef tells a story of a god-man who died, was buried, was resurrected, and still helps his people. Amadou realizes that the story is not very different from his father's story of the water god, Nommo, who brought fire, iron, and grain to the Dogon people.

Amadou has already learned to speak French in the village school. He has talked to tourists who come to visit the Dogon people. Two worlds are calling to Amadou. Though his father wishes Amadou to become a blacksmith, it is Amadou who must finally make the choice.

Opposite: Dogon millet fields in the valley below the cliffs. Nearly everyone in Amadou's village works in the fields.

Inna loves going with her grandmother to this large outdoor market in Bamako.

INNA OF BAMAKO

Twelve-year-old Inna lives in a modern house on the Avenue Lyautey in the main part of Bamako. Her father works as a technical adviser for the Malian Office of Tourism, and her mother is a sales clerk at the pharmacy in Bamako.

Inna's family is not rich, but with both her mother and father working, the family has a comfortable home with many modern conveniences. Inna's grandmother lives with them; she cleans the house, does the marketing and laundry, and helps Inna's mother with the cooking.

Inna is in the seventh grade at one of the fundamental, or elementary, schools in Bamako. She studies civics, French, geography, history, mathematics, and natural sciences, but she likes physical education best. Inna hopes to attend the normal school (teacher training school) in three years and major in English. After graduation, she could teach grades six through nine in one of Mali's many second-cycle elementary schools. But first she must pass the very difficult admission examination after she receives her fundamental education diploma.

The normal school Inna wants to attend is a new school located in Badalabougou, one of the suburbs of Bamako. Besides English, she will also take physical education, art education, and the general education requirements.

Inna enjoys going with her grandmother to the large open market in downtown Bamako. Most of all, she enjoys going to the zoo with her uncle. Inna likes the elephants and giraffes, but her favorite animals are the zebras, which came to the Bamako Zoo from Tanzania in East Africa. Inna has never seen any of these animals outside the zoo, though her uncle says that there are a few wild elephants and giraffes in Mali.

Occasionally, when all the guides and hostesses are busy, Inna's father takes groups of tourists to Mopti and Timbuktu. Once Inna went along. She was excited about the long drive to Mopti and the airplane flight to Timbuktu. She was fascinated by the great fish market in Mopti and was as interested as any tourist in hearing her father explain how the Bozo fishermen caught their tons of fish. In Timbuktu she marveled at the camel caravans and had her picture taken with other tourists in front of the ancient mosque.

Since visiting these ancient and historical towns of Mali, Inna has become very much interested in the past glories of her country. Almost every week, she goes to the National Museum and gazes silently at the many art works that belong to Mali's long and glorious history.

MAHAMANE OF THE SAHARA

Mahamane and his family earn their living in northern Mali on the edge of the great Sahara. In many ways, their life has changed very little from that of their ancestors hundreds of years ago. Mahamane's people are the Tuareg, who now number less than 250,000. The Tuareg are split into many small groups of wandering herdsmen. Each group is made up of members of different tribes who have been split up since the early nineteenth century. Mahamane's tribe is the Tenguereguif. His mother is the great granddaughter of the famous Tuareg leader, Chebboum, who defeated a French force in 1894 near Timbuktu.

Mahamane is proud of being a member of such a famous *inochar,* or warrior tribe. He also respects other tribesmen who are Muslim teachers. But he looks down on the tent servants who work for his family; they are the *imrad*—vassals who pay tribute to his family for protection and use of water and pasture. He thinks they are less intelligent than his warrior family.

Though Mahamane knows that Allah made all men equal, he is taught that the lower classes with darker skins are expected to be respectful and obedient to him, because he is an inochar. Mahamane expects to become the next leader of the group when his uncle dies.

When Mahamane was very young, he began to prepare himself for his place as leader. He knew that unless he was brave and strong, some other members of his group might take over when his uncle dies. He listened carefully to his mother's teachings—especially to the historical songs that she sings and plays on her *imzad* (a stringed instrument).

Mahamane and the rest of his group would not attend the school that the government tried to establish a few years

Mahamane and his family earn their living in northern Mali on the edge of the great Sahara Desert (below).

before near Araouane. Mahamane's mother taught him to write in their language, Tamachek, which uses the Tifinar alphabet. That seemed enough. He would have liked nothing better than to raise his camels and to continue to bring salt south from Taoudeni in the desert to sell in Timbuktu. His ancestors had always been able to live free and healthy lives wandering in search of pasture.

But for the past few years, the rains, which used to make pastures almost overnight, have not come. Mahamane's father has moved the herds farther south each year, yet many of the animals have died. Many of the imrad have gone far south into the farmlands of other groups, and most of Mahamane's mother's tent servants have also left. Even if the rains come next year, Mahamane's uncle fears that there are not enough animals left for the tribe, and without the imrad to help grow grain and other food, there will be hunger.

Mahamane may inherit the leadership of a dying tribe. Yet where will the son of a noble family find work in the already crowded towns of Mali? And how can one who has always expected others to serve him now become the servant of others for money?

But without rains the flocks and herds will die, and without them the Tuareg lifestyle is gone. Mahamane worries and watches the skies as his tribes' animals weaken. Sometimes he thinks that his people will have to go to Timbuktu for food. Yet how can a warrior's son beg? Mahamane asks.

Mahamane's Tuareg family has been bringing salt slabs from the Sahara to Timbuktu for many, many generations. From Timbuktu, the salt is transported by canoe to the great port of Mopti on the Niger River (below).

Mali Yesterday

THE EARLIEST MALIANS

The Sahara has not always been desert. Once it was lush and verdant; grass and occasional trees covered the land. The many lakes provided water for man and animals. Fish, game, clams, and wild food were easy to find. In paleolithic times (*paleo* means "very old" and *lithic* means "stone"), hunters using stone tools roamed these grasslands. At least sixty thousand years ago, some of these hunters had reached what is now the stark desert of northern Mali.

By 40,000 B.C. fire-using hunters and gatherers were settling farther south on the edge of Mali's forest. During this period, the Sahara was a better watered area. But gradually over the last seven thousand years, it has become drier. Part of the cause was less rainfall, but man was also partly responsible. Hunting groups often burned the brush and tall grasses to drive out the hunted animals. Herdsmen with grazing cattle and goats have further diminished the green cover in the last six thousand years or more.

By 4000 B.C., people were unable to live by hunting and herding alone. The population had grown and so had the desert; there were too many people and there was too little space. The people gradually moved south into the lush inner Niger delta, thus swelling the population there. In time, most of the animals were killed off. When the people were unable to support the larger populations by hunting and fishing, they began the difficult task of farming.

These expanding farming populations in Mali developed their own crops and agricultural techniques. The agricultural revolution and the discovery of iron caused many changes. With iron hoes and axes, the farmers could move farther south into the forested areas and cultivate more grain on the open plains. When the camel was introduced from Arabia in about 300 A.D., trade grew much faster. Grain surpluses and a larger population allowed specialists to practice their crafts. The simple agricultural villages began to evolve into city-states and trading kingdoms.

GREAT KINGDOMS

Three of the greatest West African empires existed largely in present-day Mali. Here fish from the Niger River, rich grasslands, and sufficient rain allowed larger populations to come together in towns. The Ghana Empire, the first of these great empires, existed from the seventh to the eleventh centuries. Kumbi Saleh, Ghana's capital, was located in modern-day Mauritania, but the empire controlled large areas of trade in modern-day Mali.

The Mali Empire lasted from the thirteenth to the sixteenth centuries. Its capital, Niani, was located in present-day Guinea, on the trade routes between the Wangara gold fields (near Siguiri) and the northern trading city of Timbuktu. Songhai, the last of the great kingdoms, had its greatest power in the fifteenth and sixteenth centuries. Gao, its capital, was a trade crossroads from the north and south.

These three empires prospered largely because they were able to control the trade from the Mediterranean Sea to forest

When camels (below) were introduced to Mali from Arabia in about 300 A.D., trade began to increase rapidly.

MARK LA POINTE

lands south of the Sahara. Salt mined in the Sahara and products made in North African and European shops were brought south and traded for African products such as gold, ivory, and slaves.

African gold contributed to the wealth of Genoa and Venice and helped make these cities world traders during the Middle Ages. Portuguese explorers attempting to discover a direct route to this gold sailed down Africa's west coast in the fifteenth century. Once the Portuguese were able to get the gold in trade along the African coast, they could continue to sail around Africa to trade in India.

Many great cities grew up in Mali as a result of the trade across the desert and also because of the Muslim teachers who came south along the trade routes. Three of these cities—Jenne, Gao, and Timbuktu—still remain. Jenne and Timbuktu became important Muslim learning centers during the period of the great empires. The reputation of their teachers and libraries attracted hundreds of students— at a time when most Europeans were unable to read or write.

Desert traders had brought the Islamic religion to Mali before the eleventh century. Some rulers of the Mali and Songhai empires helped Muslim teachers and travelers. In fact, much of these empires' history has been passed down in the writings of the Arab visitors. Muslim influence on the kingdom's law, government, and values was very great.

MALI EMPIRE

The actual history of modern Mali began with the fall of the Ghana Empire in 1076. Part of the Ghana Empire's army fled southeast into Mali. Mounted and well armed, these warrior groups established themselves as kings in the small villages of the region. At first, the newcomers were welcomed as protectors and as a source of rare goods from the north. One of the kingdoms, the Sosso, rose to a position of dominance over the other kingdoms by forcibly recruiting local Malinke soldiers into its army. Sosso was able to capture much of the former empire of Ghana.

The small southern Malinke kingdom, which had grown up under local leadership, began to resist the Sosso. A number of revolts were crushed, but under the leadership of Sundiata, the Malinke forces defeated the Sosso ruler, Sumanguru, in 1231 at Kirina. This victory established the Mali Empire.

The Mali Empire, like the Songhai Empire that followed it, was a highly organized and centralized state. The emperor

Jenne and Timbuktu became important Muslim learning centers during the period of the great empires. The Koranic school at Jenne (left) is still an important Muslim seat of learning.

25

had absolute authority, yet Islamic law and the traditional authority of heads of the royal family kept most emperors from gaining too much control. Because revolts against harsh rule were common, no emperor lasted long unless he was good to his people. The emperor had direct control of a certain area; outside that area were conquered kingdoms. All that was expected of these border kingdoms was a *tribute*, or a payment in goods or services. Rulers in these areas often wanted to avoid paying tribute. The only way the emperor could collect was to send his army. Thus, Mali's great emperor, Mansa Kankan Musa, like most other rulers, took hostages from the border kingdoms. Sons of rulers were held to be sure their fathers would pay their taxes and remain obedient. For this reason, the empires of West Africa usually declined under weak emperors.

In 1325 Mansa Musa spread the fame of the Mali Empire throughout the world when he took sixty thousand followers with him on a pilgrimage to the Muslim holy city in Arabia. Mansa Musa distributed so much gold during a short stay in Cairo that the market was depressed for years!

When Mansa Musa died in 1332, he left behind an enormous empire that extended from the Atlantic coast far east to the Niger River. The empire extended from the forest in the south to the desert in the north. Mansa Musa was succeeded by his brother, Sulaiman. In 1353, Mali was visited by a Muslim geographer, Ibn Battuta, who wrote: "The people of Mali are seldom unjust and dislike injustice. There is complete security in their country. Travelers and inhabitants have no fear of robbers or men of violence."

Unfortunately, after Sulaiman's death, Mansa Djata came to the throne. A very bad ruler, he sold royal jewels and rare gold nuggets for his own foolish spending. Further troubles followed, and by 1468 the empire of Mali was no longer a great power.

SONGHAI EMPIRE

Songhai regained its independence from a declining Mali under the leadership of Ali Kolon and Salman Nar. Gradually, by the fifteenth century, Songhai became the most centralized of the three great West African empires. It had a permanent army, regular taxation, and officials appointed directly by the emperor. Yet rather than giving to the areas it ruled, it took from them; many small kingdoms soon became unhappy with the empire. An invasion by a Moroccan army caused the small

Opposite: The tomb of Askin at Gao. By the time Askin became emperor of the Songhai Empire in 1493, the empire was no longer a great power.

26

These Bambara hunters are descendants of the Bambara who created the states of Ségou and Kaarta in the seventeenth century.

kingdoms to break away from the strong arm of Songhai rule.

In 1591 Gao fell to the Moroccans, and with it fell the trade routes of the western Sahara. Without a strong empire joining the Sahara trade routes to the forest and southern supplies, the gold trade could not continue profitably. Also, European ships were offering a market on the coast. Saharan trade was becoming less important.

PERIOD OF TRANSITION

After Songhai had defeated Mali in the competition for the trade across the Sahara, the mansas of Mali ruled a steadily shrinking state. A great Songhai emperor, Sunni Ali, captured Timbuktu in 1468,

cutting off Mali's links to North Africa. By 1500 neither Mali nor Songhai could control the western lands near the Atlantic. Tuareg nomads raided from the desert. Trade was difficult because the great empires could not protect travelers. After the Moroccans conquered Songhai, they found that they could not keep the empire going. Soon the area split into many small quarreling groups.

With the trade, cities, and schools of the great empires gone, the impact of Islam became less important. The Bambara people, who lived in small farming communities along the Niger Valley south of Timbuktu, created two states, Ségou and Kaarta. According to legend, two brothers, Barama and Nia N'golo, formed warrior bands to protect their villages against the bandit bands that had increased after the fall of the Songhai Empire. Soon the brothers gathered the most powerful force in the valley, sometimes by raiding weaker neighbors. The son of one of these brothers, Kaladian Koulibali, attempted to rule an area that stretched along the Niger River from Timbuktu to the west of Bamako. But he was unable to establish a lasting kingdom. When he died in the late seventeenth century, his war leaders began to fight among themselves.

Not until the reign of Mamari Koulibali, a descendant of Barama N'golo, did Ségou become the capital of a real empire. Under Mamari's rule, by 1730 Ségou was a strongly fortified city and a center of trade. Mamari commanded an army of war captives and young Bambara men and had a fleet of canoes on the Niger River.

Unfortunately, Mamari quarreled with the descendants of Nia N'golo. After some violence, Nia N'golo's surviving descendants moved northwest and built a lesser kingdom called Kaarta, with its capital at Nioro. With the death of Mamari, fighting once again broke out between the war leaders. Never fully united, these kingdoms lasted only until more united Muslim powers arose.

RESTORATION OF MUSLIM POWER

By the beginning of the nineteenth century, the Muslim people of West Africa, like those near the Mediterranean, had in-directly begun to feel the pressure of European expansion. Mungo Park, an explorer, had reached the area in 1806. Also, in what is now Niger and Nigeria, Uthman dan Fodio had declared a Muslim holy war *(jihad)* against the Hausa ruling classes. Dan Fodio felt that the Hausa were mistreating his people and not acting like good Muslims.

In the Macina (a rich farming area west of the Niger River), Muslim people were especially angered. Here the Muslims wanted to get rid of their *ardo* (Fulbé leader) because they felt that he was only a puppet in the hands of the non-Muslim rulers of Ségou.

Ahmadou Barry, a young Muslim scholar who had studied under Uthman dan Fodio, had come to believe that good Muslims could not live under a non-Muslim ruler. Thus, in 1819, with enough followers to throw off the ardo's rule, he set up a truly Muslim state with its capital at Hamdullahi. Ahmadou established an orderly and well-governed state based on Islamic law. At Ahmadou's death, his rule passed to his son and later to his grandson. Not until 1862 did his kingdom fall. When it did fall, it fell to another Muslim reform movement.

In 1826 another young Muslim scholar, Al-Hajj ("the pilgrim") Umar had come through Ahmadou's kingdom. On his way home to Senegal, he had married Uthman dan Fodio's daughter. Moving west, Umar began to teach a simple, devout form of Islam which enrolled men into a brotherhood called the Tijaniyya.

He gathered followers for ten years — until the almami (Muslim ruler) of the area expelled him as a disruptive force. Umar fled with his followers, purchased guns, and began his attempt to reform people by force in a holy war. He was successful against Kaarta in 1854 and Ségou in 1861. Finally in 1862 Umar defeated Ahmadou's grandson in Macina, justifying his attack on a fellow Muslim state by claiming that Macina had helped the non-Muslim state of Ségou defend itself.

By the time Umar died in 1864, his empire was already crumbling. Umar's son, Ahmad, was attacked in Ségou shortly after Umar's death. At the same time, Ahmad's brothers were looking for ways to set themselves up as separate princes, and the French armies were moving in from Senegal. In 1890 Ahmad's forces were pushed out of Nioro, the capital of Kaarta, by black Senegalese and French troops. Soon Ségou fell. By 1893 Ahmad was forced to flee to his mother's homeland in Nigeria, where he died five years later.

FRENCH CONQUEST

The conquest of present-day Mali began in 1854, when the French government in Dakar, Senegal, under Louis Faidherbe, began to send spies as far west as Ségou. The next year, a battle between paid French troops and Umar's followers took place at Fort Medina (on the border of modern Senegal and Mali). Umar's death, Faidherbe's return to France in 1865, and the Prussian invasion of France brought about a calm period for a while. But the French Empire was on its way to the conquest of most of West Africa.

In 1879 J. S. Gallieni's appointment as political director in Senegal marked France's final push to control a large African empire. Two years later, Gallieni traveled to Ségou to sign a treaty with Ahmad; at the same time, he tried to gain support of the non-Muslim Bambara against Ahmad. The French moved in to establish forts at Kita and Bamako. In 1888 the railroad from Dakar was built as far as Bafoulabé, on its way to Kayes and the Niger River.

Ahmad, faced with internal revolts and lack of supplies, still offered strong resistance to the French advance. In 1890 Ahmad's forces defended Ségou against a strong French attack under General Archinard. But the French finally destroyed the walls with artillery, and Ahmad fled with his followers. In Jenne and Bandiagara, Ahmad's forces continued to fight bravely for as long as they could against the superior armaments of the French. France's conquest of this empire proved

In 1885, Fort Medina at Kayes (opposite) was the site of a battle between French troops and Umar's followers. The fort is now used as a primary school.

costly to them in both men and supplies. But the French were unable to occupy the rest of Mali without a struggle. The Bambara soon realized that the French were coming to stay. In 1890 the Bambara staged a fierce but unsuccessful revolt against the better-armed and better-organized French troops.

RESISTANCE

At this time, a Malinke leader named Samori Touré was also fighting the French armies. As a teenager, Samori had served as a soldier for the local ruler in order to free his mother, who had been taken as a captive. Later, as a traveling merchant, he had visited places that were deeply involved in the jihads of Umar, Ahmadou, and others. As a Malinke, Samori also knew of Mali's glorious past. Strongly affected by these experiences, Samori decided that a new Muslim state was necessary to bring together all the small, warring Malinke states in the area.

Samori spent thirty years building up a group of followers and uniting the towns and villages south of Umar's empire. He was able to create a strong, unified state by using a common belief in Islam to unite the people. As the leader of an independent Malinke kingdom, he sought alliances with the French, the British, and other African states.

Samori soon found out, however, that the French wanted more than peaceful trade: they wanted to rule all of West Africa. So in the 1880s Samori started to fight the French.

Though the French signed a treaty in 1887 allowing Samori control over a large part of northeast Guinea and southwest Mali, fighting continued. An alliance in 1890 with Ahmad, who was still holding out in Bandiagara, came too late to help Samori. The French had more guns, and Samori's men were unable to continue to fight and feed their families forever. Driven east along the Mali-Ivory Coast border, Samori continued to fight a guerilla war against the French until he was finally captured by trickery in 1898.

FRENCH OCCUPATION

A number of other small trading states offered some resistance to France in the late nineteenth century. But with few exceptions, the French had succeeded in occupying most of Mali by the 1890s.

In 1893 the French took Timbuktu with the help of a small gunboat on the Niger River. But the town was liberated by Tuareg forces, who destroyed a French force the following year. The French, however, were able to retake Timbuktu later that year.

The creation of a French government of the Upper Senegal at Kayes in 1895, the capture of Samori in 1898, and the end of all large-scale resistance in the trading towns of Mali made French rule dominant.

This Bobo village near Ségou was the site of a 1919 revolution of the Bobo people. This was one of the last revolts against the French in Mali.

FRENCH PRESENCE

French occupation of Mali was an important factor in the nation's modern history. From 1857, when French forces first crossed swords with Al-Hajj Umar's soldiers, until the 1890s, when the forces of Samori and Ahmad were defeated, French presence in the area was that of an advancing army. The French military began to pour in from the Senegal River and, by train, from Dakar. Smaller forces from coastal bases in Guinea and the Ivory Coast also attempted to gain control of the land. By the outbreak of World War I, African armed resistance in modern Mali had been completely destroyed.

From the middle of the nineteenth century, the French had dreamed of conquering Timbuktu and the West African gold trade. They believed that tremendous wealth still lay in the territory of the great West Africa empires. The French went so far as to make plans for a trans-Saharan railroad to connect the planned African empire with metropolitan France across the Mediterranean. Unfortunately, France's military conquests in Mali never resulted in the wealth that many French believed existed in the savanna and sahelian regions. For many years, the trans-Saharan trade had been reduced to a mere trickle; Mali's potential was in agriculture. The French won battles, as had other African conquerors, but the French never found the economic opportunities or wealth that they sought.

What drove the French armies on was not just the desire for gold. The military leaders were seeking glory, personal hon-

or, and a chance to prove themselves. Few French citizens were interested in an African empire, especially if ruling it would cost them money. Few Africans in Mali wanted to be conquered by a French army.

COLONIAL RULE

After the French had conquered Mali, their immediate problem was how to rule the territory. Though the French had kept other European countries from grabbing the land first, the cost of keeping this control proved to be high.

French military conquest had overthrown the African governments, but France had neither the men nor the money to put a French administrator in each village. Often the military chose leaders from the African population, but this system was not very successful. If the chosen African was capable and accepted by the local people, he soon opposed French authority. If he was unacceptable to the African population, the French were forced to step in anyway. Unless they had some real power, the French-appointed rulers were little more than puppets, and were not able to rule very effectively.

Kayes became the capital of an Upper Senegal-Niger colony and Bamako the capital of the colony of the French Sudan. There was no room for African participation in this French-controlled government. But educated Africans constantly demanded the rights and privileges consistent with French democracy.

AFRICAN POWER

The governor of the French Sudan was a Frenchman, who was under the authority of a governor-general in Dakar; he, in turn, had to answer to the Minister of Colonies in France. Decisions were imposed from above, and Africans were left almost totally without power. Gradually, however, some Africans achieved a little power. In a few areas, such as Macina, Fulbé noble families maintained power by pretending to accept French authority. To obtain power in the early years, they had to help the French. In Mali, this meant collecting taxes and providing men to work for the French. Thus, profits and opportunities for individual Africans were usually at the expense of fellow Africans.

In time, a small number of interpreters, teachers, office workers, and African paramedics (doctors' assistants) were trained to help the French. But this group never amounted to more than 5 percent of the population. Africans who served in the French army and on the railroad gradually came to feel that they should have some voice in the running of their own affairs.

A few Africans were allowed to become French citizens, but several conditions had to be met for an African to be considered for citizenship. He had to have worked for the French for ten years, had to have been French-educated, and had to have served in the French army. In other words, an African man who wanted equal rights had to give up his African lifestyle and become, in essence, a black Frenchman. In any case, by 1938 only a couple of hundred Africans in the French Sudan had become citizens.

For most Africans, forced labor, taxation without representation, army service, and arbitrary French justice was the ordinary way of life until the 1940s. For "talking back" to a Frenchman, an African could be imprisoned for two weeks (later reduced to five days). Africans began to wish that there was something they could do to better their condition.

WORLD WAR II

During the war, Malians faced even greater hardships. Many young Malian men were drafted to protect the French from Hitler's invasion. When France fell to the Germans, West Africa came under the rule of the Hitler-controlled Vichy government. Shortages of manufactured goods grew as the German authorities made more demands on conquered France. The few Africans who resisted the Vichy government were shot. Some Malians migrated into nearby countries, but most continued to live as they always had. For most Africans, it made little difference whether their lives were indirectly controlled from Berlin or from Paris.

In 1943, after the French National Liberation group regained control of the West African colonies, Africans were forced to contribute their efforts to helping the French defeat the Germans. Hundreds of Malians served in the French armed forces. At home in Mali, Africans built the dams and bridges, grew the rice, supplied the food, and paid taxes to help the French. Because of truck and gasoline shortages, Africans were forced to carry supplies on their heads. In return, the Malians were promised a better life.

AFTER THE WAR

When the war was over, many colonial people throughout the world felt that the fine words about a better world, which the Allied leaders had proclaimed, should also apply to them. In 1944 French officials from French West Africa and Equatorial Africa attended a conference in Brazzaville, Congo. Plans were made to alter colonial rule.

The constitution drawn up after the war made Mali an overseas territory. In theory, all Africans in the territory became citizens, rather than subjects. Forced labor was abolished, an elected assembly was set up, and a federal council for all of French West Africa was established. Mali was also allowed to elect deputies to the French National Assembly and Senate.

The problem was that neither the Malian Assembly nor the federal council in Dakar could make laws. They were merely advisory councils, and were often ignored by the French. Different laws continued to be applied for French citizens of French status (usually white) and French citizens of local status (almost always black).

Not until 1956, when Mali was granted a form of internal self-government, were Africans given equal voting rights. The territorial assembly was allowed to elect a Council of Ministers, which served as the executive branch, under the French-appointed governor. The minister with the highest number of votes became vice-president.

INDEPENDENCE

Long before the French government was ready to grant free elections, a new political party, led by Modibo Keita, had been formed to elect members to the territorial and federal assemblies. With the help of progressive French politicians, this Sudanese Union Party (US) grew from a handful of teachers and labor leaders in 1946 to Mali's only political party in 1959.

During the colony's first elections in 1946, French authorities used their power and the traditional ruler's help to elect their candidates. When a group of African leaders from French West Africa met in Bamako in October of that year to establish the African Democratic Party (RDA), the pro-French candidate was defeated as the RDA Malian delegate. Instead, Modibo Keita was elected as the French Sudan delegate for the RDA. The conservative pro-French forces continued to hold some power in Mali until the 1957 National Assembly elections. By then, the majority of the population had gradually come to support Keita's Sudanese Union Party.

De Gaulle came to power in France amid the crisis caused by the Algerian Revolution. To avoid other revolutions, he called for a referendum, in which French African colonies could choose between independence free from any French control or they could become part of a French community with total internal self-government but French control of all external affairs.

Mali voted to remain within the community. As the Sudanese Republic, it joined in 1959 with Senegal to form the Mali Federation. This federation became independent of France as a unit in June of 1960. Two months later, Senegal and Mali split apart; on September 22, 1960, the Sudanese Republic officially became the Republic of Mali by vote of the representative assembly.

Mali Today

AFTER INDEPENDENCE

Modibo Keita, born in Bamako in 1915, graduated from a French teacher-training school in Dakar. He was elected mayor of Bamako in 1956 and president of the territorial assembly two years later. In January of 1956, he was elected deputy from the Sudan (now present-day Mali) to the French National Assembly. As head of the Sudanese Union Party, Keita led the colony to independence in 1960. Elected president of the Republic of Mali after independence, he served in this capacity for eight years.

Immediately after independence, Keita requested the recall of all French troops serving in Mali, the return of Malian troops serving in French armed forces, and a halt to French nuclear testing in the Sahara. With the Dakar-Niger railroad closed due to the split with Senegal and faced with a decline in French aid, Mali turned for help to the Soviet Union and China. A state-owned trading company, SOMIEX (Malian Society of Imports and Exports), tried to sell Mali's goods and buy imports on the world market. SOMIEX found this task difficult because France and other Western European countries, as well as the United States, consistently snubbed Mali.

During the first eight years after independence, Keita attempted an overambitious expenditure, resulting in a several-million-dollar debt. Thus, the economy declined. The Mali government stated that it would create a separate currency in September of 1962, but this caused unrest among the country's business interests. Conspiracy trials followed in which two former pro-French politicians were ac-

President Moussa Traoré of Mali has a strong position of leadership in his country.

MINISTRY OF INFORMATION

President Traoré with President Moctar Ouldada of Mauritania.

MINISTRY OF INFORMATION

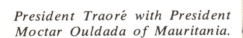

cused of plotting against the government; the politicians were condemned to death. Unrest and difficulties followed, yet Keita retained the support of most Malians. On May 6, 1967, the Mali government devalued the currency by 50 percent and returned to the French franc zone. For people on fixed incomes, such as government employees, this meant their income was cut in half.

COUP D'ÉTAT

In November of 1968, a group of young army officers arrested President Keita and seized control of the government. Keita was imprisoned, and Lieutenant Moussa Traoré became the leader of the country as chief of state and president of the Military Committee of National Liberation.

Traoré, born in 1936 in Kayes, was once an officer in the French army; later he was in charge of officer's training in the Malian army. Traoré has attempted to maintain a middle course between East and West in the years since the military take-over. Faced with a serious student strike in April of 1969 and an attempt to bring Modibo Keita back to power in August of 1969, Traoré took over as president of government functions in September of that year and settled into a strong position of leadership.

Since 1968, the government has attempted to develop a plan that is compatible with Mali's resources. The three-year plan put forth attempted to increase the country's total output about 20 percent by 1973, to hold down the growth of imports to 4 percent, and to increase exports by 10 percent a year. To decrease foreign assistance as much as possible, one fourth of the development budget was to be spent on agriculture. This plan failed, however, because of severe drought during the three years of the plan.

GOVERNMENT

Presently Mali is governed by a well-established military government. Officers and troops serve in key areas as governmental administrators. When the military first took over, it promised to return power to civilian hands as soon as conditions for democracy were right. Among the military government's prime objectives in its first year was the creation of a new constitution. The constitution was to be written in consultation with a wide representation of the population and submitted in a referendum. This was to be followed by a popular election for the president and National Assembly. Free movement of people and merchandise were to be guaranteed, but price regulation was seen as necessary. Current agriculture and transportation problems made this last item indispensible.

Daily governmental affairs since 1968 have continued to operate with little disruption. The judicial branch of government continues to function, and the civil service positions remain largely untouched. The National Assembly was dissolved in 1967 during a cultural revolution, and the only deliberative body now is the Committee of National Liberation, with Traoré as its head.

INTERNATIONAL RELATIONS

Malian international politics is largely determined by the country's geographic position. Traoré has attempted to maintain excellent relations with neighboring countries, since Mali has no direct access to the sea. Mali belongs to a group of states along the Senegal River that attempts to coordinate the use of the river for power, irrigation, and transportation.

Mali is a member of the Organization of African Unity (OAU). The Mali government's principle foreign position is one of overall nonalignment with any power.

EDUCATION

Mali has made great strides in education since independence. The country has a long heritage of Koranic schools and Muslim education, which dates back to the thirteenth and fourteenth centuries when the Muslim teachers and scholars of Jenne, Timbuktu, and Gao attracted students from throughout West and North Africa.

Today the nation of Mali has made a very definite commitment to provide a meaningful education for as many Malian students as possible. Faced with a limited budget, Mali has attempted to concentrate on fundamental education. The training of secondary school teachers, administrators, engineers, medical personnel, and agricultural extension workers has also been given top educational priority.

Agricultural education is offered in ninety rural centers. There are three apprentice centers at Samanko, M'Pesoba, and San, a school of veterinary assistants at Bamako, and the Rural Polytechnical Institute at Katibougou.

Fundamental school education extends to the ninth grade and is divided into two cycles. During the first five years general courses are taught. Courses during the following four years lead to some specialization. At present, fundamental school education is available to only 20 percent of the population.

About eight hundred Malian students study overseas in France and Eastern Europe, and about a thousand students are enrolled in secondary, technical, and professional schools, such as the National Schools of Engineers, National Institute of Arts, and Secondary School of Health.

Schools range from simply mud-and-tin village schools to schools with modern facilities. In all of the schools, the desire to learn is great. Young Malians are the hope of the future, and educational opportunity is one of the most important investments the country can make.

Opposite: Education in Mali has recently been expanded to include some adults such as these, who are attending a literacy class at Moribabougou, near Bamako.

As part of a program of rural development, the government of Mali has opened several agricultural training centers. *Above:* Students attend class at Centre Apprenticage Agricole. *Below:* Cattle at the centre are housed in this modern corral. *Opposite:* A student places newly made bricks under a protective covering to dry.

Natural Treasures

ANIMAL LIFE

Even though Mali is more than six hundred miles from the nearest port, the country exports tons of dried and smoked fish each year. There is a variety of good fishing in the Niger and Bani rivers as well as on Lakes Débo, Faguibine, and Horo in the inland delta of the Niger. Motorized boats can be rented at Mopti and a few other places on the river. The Capitaine, a large fish, is greatly sought after because of its delicious flavor. The rivers are dangerous, however, as they are home to a large number of hippopotamuses and crocodiles.

Though Mali is not a big-game hunter's paradise, there are a variety of animals and birds in the country. Scattered throughout the less-inhabited areas of the savanna, especially northeast of Mopti and along the southern border, are some larger animals such as giraffes, Derby elands, elephants, and a few larger antelope. Throughout the country are baboons, egrets, daries, and francolin (a kind of partridge).

Three types of poisonous snakes are found in Mali: the mamba, viper, and cobra, as well as a number of non-poisonous pythons, some of which grow to more than ten feet long.

Mali is rich in livestock; there are more cattle in Mali than there are people. Sheep and goats are raised almost everywhere but pigs are found only among the few

There is excellent fishing in many rivers and lakes in Mali.
Opposite: Fishing with a cast net on the Niger River.

47

non-Muslims. Chickens are allowed to run free. Many of the more wealthy northern people have horses, and camels are kept by people living near Gao. Donkeys are not uncommon as a means of transporting both people and goods throughout the country.

MINERAL RESOURCES

With few exceptions, Mali's mineral resources are almost totally untapped. There is a good possibility that oil lies beneath the Sahara. Some minor bauxite deposits have been found in the Kita region southwest of Bamako. With a 50 percent alumina content, these bauxite deposits may be valuable in the future. In the same area are also deposits of relatively low-grade iron ore.

Other minerals that have already been discovered are manganese, lithium, phosphates, and copper. Small traces of zinc, lead, tin, and uranium have also been noted. Salt, the ancient and still highly valued item of trade in West Africa, is still transported by camel caravans from Taoudeni in the far northern desert.

Lime (used for cement), marble, and granite are mined in Mali and used for building. Kaolin, found in a number of deposits, is used for pottery and ceramics.

Mali will perhaps never be a rich, industrialized country. Yet many of the country's resources are only beginning to be realized. With foreign technical and financial aid, Mali has a good hope of survival as an independent nation.

Left: This huge fish was caught in Ségou Harbor. Opposite: Donkeys are a common means of transportation in Mali.

MINISTRY OF INFORMATION

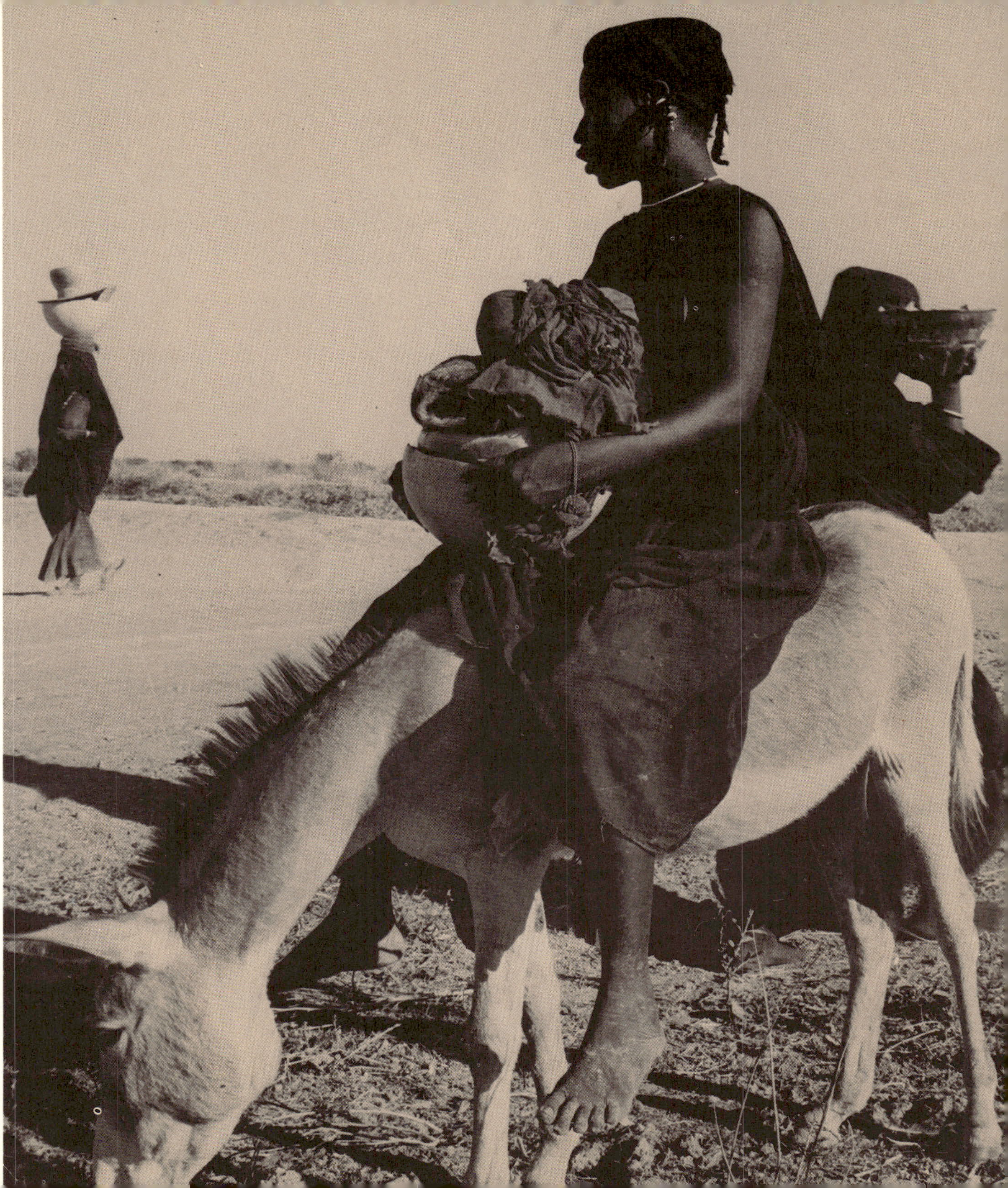

MINISTRY OF INFORMATION

The People Live in Mali

PAST PRESTIGE

A young person in Mali is never far removed from the history of his people. Throughout the countryside, *griots* (historians and praise-singers) are always ready to recite the tales of yesterday's heroes. The stories of the kings, princes, and warriors of the ancient kingdoms of Mali, Songhai, and Ghana are part of the everyday world of most young Malians.

But Malian children do not learn about their heritage only through the folk traditions. Muslim teachers tell the stories of holy men and pilgrims. More than 60 percent of the population is Muslim; this common religious heritage helps unite the country's many different languages and ethnic groups.

A common pride in the country is one of Mali's educational goals. A number of national history books are used in the schools; these books are full of praise for the brave men and women who fought when the French came to take over the land.

With all of the nation's past glories, it is sometimes difficult for young Malians to remember that even the great heroes of the past were real human beings with both strengths and weaknesses. Keeping this fact in mind, however, might help young

More than 60 percent of the population of Mali is Muslim.
Opposite: Muslims at prayer in front of the mosque at Mopti.

This Bambara farmer has a daba on his shoulder. A daba is a hoe, and is used by the farmer to till his fields.

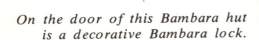

On the door of this Bambara hut is a decorative Bambara lock.

A bush fire early in the dry season fills the village of Bafoulabé with smoke.

people to avoid overreliance on any one great leader as the savior of the country. In this way, perhaps the "cult of personality" that grew up around the first president, Modibo Keita, can be avoided.

Perhaps the greatest heroes of Mali, past and present, are not the great kings and rulers, but the ordinary people. It was the hard work of the men, women, and children in thousands of peasant villages throughout the land that supported the armies of the great kingdoms. Today, as Mali seeks to develop economically, it is again the rural populations of Mali who are the heroes of this struggle. The living sense of the past helps unite the farming peoples of Mali to persevere and create a better way of life for their children. Their

deep attachment to the land of their ancestors and their battles against difficult farming conditions is the real story of Mali.

A NATION OF VILLAGES

The great majority of people in Mali have always lived in small villages. Today only about twelve thousand people, or 7 percent of the population, live in towns. Scattered throughout the land are small clusters of straw-roofed houses. Each small cluster, or village, is made up of a number of large families. Though there are many different groups of people, including Bambara, Malinke, and Dogon,

53

who speak different languages and have different traditions, they all have very similar lifestyles.

Families in Mali are extended families; they include grandparents, aunts, and uncles as well as parents, brothers, and sisters. Since many of the men who head the families have more than one wife, extended families can become quite large. In fact, sometimes a whole village is made up of only one extended family.

In all villages, a council of family heads, usually directed by the head of one of the oldest or largest families, decides what work is to be done and what part of the village land is to be farmed by each family group. Most of these village groups are basically self-supporting units with little need of the outside world, except for a few trade goods. In recent years, however, radios, bicycles, schools, and political activity have opened the villages up more and more to outside influence.

REGIONAL VARIATIONS

There are some rural people in Mali who are not farmers. In the north, in the seasonal grasslands and oases of the Sahara, about 350,000 people live mostly by herding. These herders—Tuaregs, Moors, and others—have a long history of excellence in trade. Their camel caravans linked Mali to the Mediterranean world until recent times. But today's trucks and decline in this type of trade have put many of the old caravans out of business.

As nomadic warriors, upper-class Tuaregs and neighboring Moors share a basically independent life. In the past, lower-class people among them farmed the oases and made the few leather and metal goods that were needed. But today this way of life is dying.

Tuaregs, Moors, and Arabs brought the Islamic religion to Mali centuries ago. Today this is the main religion in Mali. Many Muslims are literate in Arabic, since this is the language of the Koran. Even non-Muslims in Mali are strongly influenced by Muslim thought and practices.

Another important group of nonfarmers are the Fulbé, who number about 750,000. They have had a great impact on Malian history. As excellent horsemen, warriors, and devout Muslims, they often imposed their rule over large areas of Mali in the past three centuries. In this way, they also helped to spread Islam.

Today some Fulbé live in small groups as cattle herdsmen. But only in the area of Macina and Nioro do they form a ruling group. Here they attempt to maintain the old ways as landlords and large-scale cattle herders. But these old ruling groups

Until recent times, Tuareg camel caravans (opposite top) linked Mali to the Mediterranean world. Today's trucks (opposite bottom) and decline in this type of trade have put many of the old caravans out of business.

UNITED NATIONS

The people of Mali.
Left: Fisherman at Mopti.
Below left: Mother and child,
Bamako.
Below right: Young Fulani
girls in the region of Mopti.
Opposite top: Young Sarakolé
girl from the Bamako area.
Opposite bottom: This woman
is selling pottery in the
main marketplace of Ségou.

UNITED NATIONS

MINISTRY OF INFORMATION

UNITED NATIONS

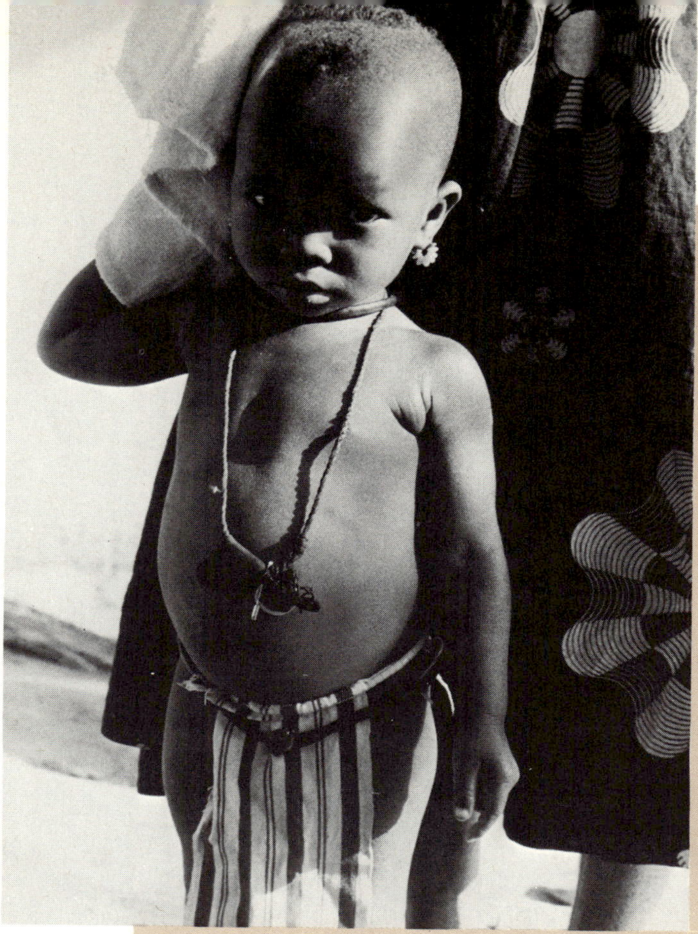

UNITED NATIONS

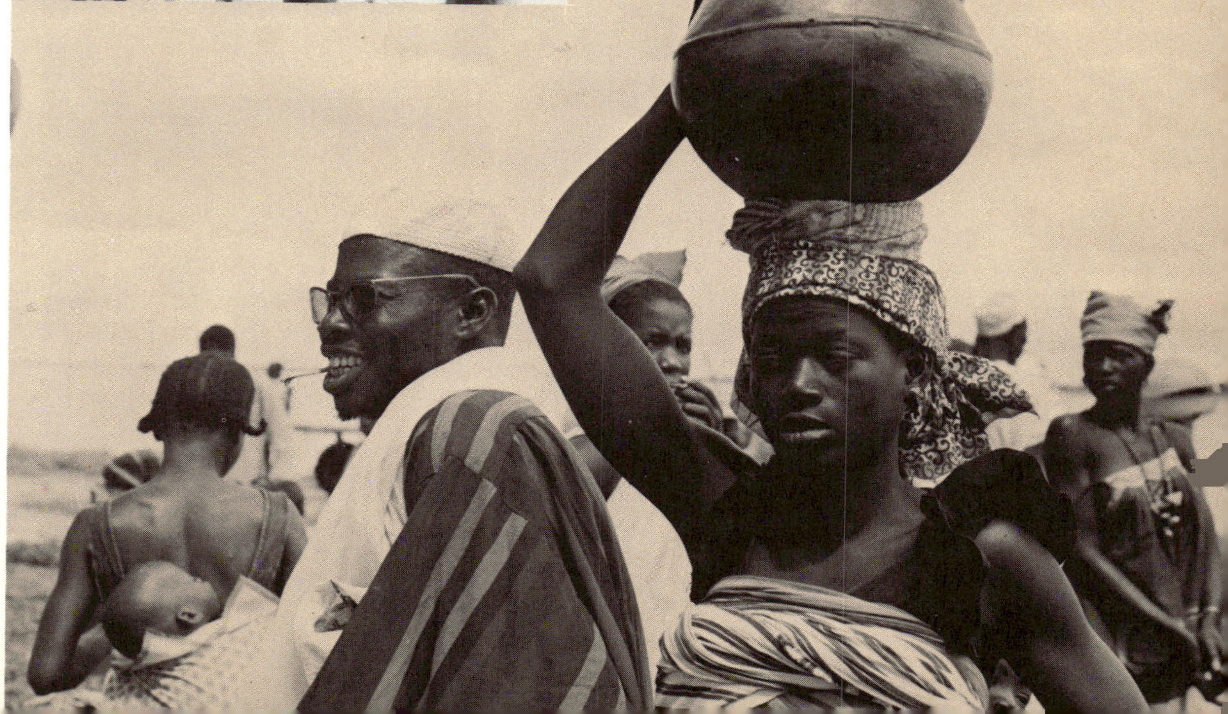

Opposite: Fish traps drying on a tree close to the Senegal River.
Above: Fishing near a major bridge on the Niger River.

are slowly being forced out of power as class and privilege give way to a more democratic government in Mali.

There are a number of other smaller groups in Mali who are not farmers. Among the more interesting of these Malians are the Bozo, the master fishermen of Mali. From Mopti to Bamako on the Niger River and from San on the Bani River, they make their living by fishing, moving up and down the river according to the demands of good fishing locations.

Their nomadic lifestyle and excellent fishing techniques are an important contribution to the economic life of Mali.

CULTURAL LIFE

Rapid modernization has not destroyed Mali's ethnic and historical traditions. African traditions are very much alive in the nation today. The National Institute of Arts conducts a fine-arts program that teaches both African and European music, drama, and painting. A vocational institute also trains young people in Malian traditional arts and crafts.

Malian scholars such as Bokar N'Dianye, Hampaté Bâ, and Dominique Traoré have published a number of oral traditions and poems. Djibril Tamsir Niane has told the story of Sundiata, the founder of the Mali Empire, in a book for American students. Young writers such as Yambo Ouloguem, the author of *The Necessity of Violence,* and Ousmane Sembene, a Senegalese film director and writer, author of *God's Bit of Wood* (a novel about both Senegal and Mali), have attempted to integrate the old and the new into a viable whole. Captain Yoro Dia-kite, the former acting president, wrote a novel published at Bamako entitled *A Friendly Hand.* A young filmmaker, Abdoulaye Seck, has won international notice with his films on human problems.

Malian poetry written in French is still too imitative of school French to be of much importance. But a few young writers have begun to use ethnic poetry as a source, and this shows promise.

The National Museum has preserved carvings and artifacts from the ethnic cultures of Mali. Even more important is the government's encouragement of the preservation of Malian dance and songs. The National Folklore Troupe of Mali has integrated into its performances the authentic dance, music, and choreography of

Writer Hampaté Bâ and his family.

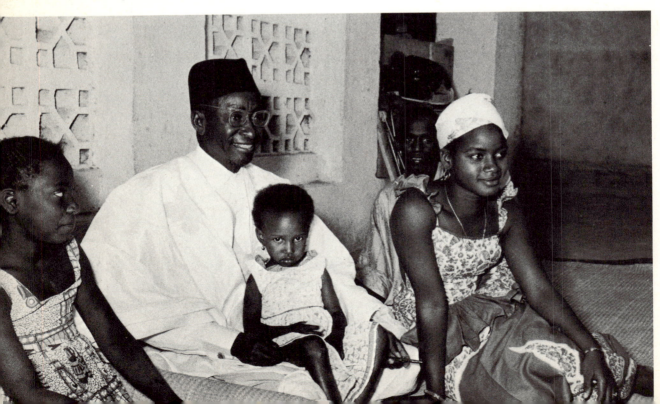

Left: This woman is weaving at the Artisan Centre in Bamako.
Below left: Sculptors at the National Institute of Art, Bamako.
Below right: Wood sculptor at work in the Artisan Centre.

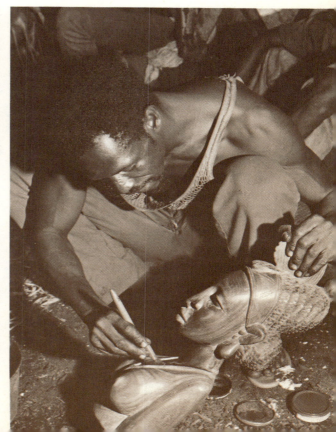

the Bambara, Senoufo, and Malinke peoples. The troupe is continuing to add materials derived from the Fulbé, Tuareg, and Dogon peoples to create a genuine national repertoire. The national radio presents traditional *cora* (a stringed instrument) and *balafon* (a sort of xylophone) music on many occasions.

A careful integration of past into present with little self-consciousness and over-styling makes the living folk culture of Mali one of the world's richest. At the same time, the national orchestra and regional bands throughout Mali play contemporary music for modern tastes. At the Institute of Fine Arts, a production of an authentic African drama can be preceded by a Molière farce. This is truly a living culture.

SOCIAL SERVICES

Mali has made progress in bringing better health care to more people. Foreign aid, especially that offered by the Catholic missions, has been put to good use. Mali has about fifty maternity clinics, more than three hundred dispensaries, ten hospitals, and about fifty social welfare centers.

There are more than one hundred doctors, more than one hundred midwives, and about twelve hundred nurses. These are certainly not enough medical workers to solve all of the nation's medical problems. But in comparison with other African countries, Mali has made great strides in improving the health of the people. With American aid, most of Mali's population has been vaccinated in a mass campaign against measles and smallpox.

The role of women in Mali has greatly increased in importance over the past ten years. By law, a woman can no longer be forced into marriage, and a woman must be at least fifteen before she can marry. Except for a relatively small number of educated women in the larger cities, most Malian women are not involved in positions of social, economic, or political power. Most village women work long hours in the fields and also take care of their homes and families. They have neither the time nor the chance for education or political involvement. For the majority of these village women, social services have only begun to help them in their most pressing needs. Education in child care, nutrition, personal hygiene, and prenatal care is insufficient throughout the country;

The National Folklore Troupe of Mali is continuing to add material from the Dogon and other peoples of Mali to create a genuine national dance repertoire. Opposite: These Dogon dancers are doing the traditional Dance of the Mask.

MINISTRY OF INFORMATION

63

improving these services is one of the primary goals of the government's social affairs branch.

In February of 1967, with the help of a number of international organizations, Mali began a campaign to eliminate illiteracy. Plans were made to train literate industrial workers to teach their fellow workers, who in turn would be taught to teach others. Thousands of farmers were to be taught elementary reading, writing, and arithmetic in Bambara by local people trained for this work and then helped to do the same for others. The government remains quite confident that the project, though slow in the beginning, will bring increasing benefits to the country in terms of increased production. The personal benefits are hard to count, but it is certain that for many the joys of reading, writing, and doing one's own calculations are very great.

The present government has taken a pragmatic and flexible approach to national growth. It seems to be making a sincere effort to face the difficulties of the future with the dignity, hard work, and quiet courage that is so typical of the Malian people. Today, if no great natural disaster interferes, the country seems destined to continue the slow but steady improvement of the nation's lifestyle.

Though Mali has begun a program to eliminate illiteracy, a large percentage of Malians still cannot read and write. This public writer has two clients who wish to have him write some letters for them.

The People Work in Mali

A LAND OF FARMERS

Mali is a land of farmers. More than 60 percent of the country's production is in agriculture. In the central plains, where rainfall is more than fifteen inches a year, Mali has a great potential in the production of cereal crops. Millet, sorghum, rice, maize (corn), and fonio (a special type of millet) are the chief cereal crops raised by the farmers for food for themselves and their families. At least 120 million acres of millet alone are planted each year.

The average farmer also plants yams, sweet potatoes, and manioc (used for tapioca). Women usually plant tomatoes, eggplant, okra, and peppers in small gardens near their houses. Other vegetables, shea nuts for oil, mangoes, oranges, and pineapples are also available in the markets in most regions.

Cotton and peanuts are Mali's two basic commercial crops. Mali hopes that someday it will be able to cultivate and export rice and sugar cane. Since rice has become the most important food grain for much of West Africa, this crop is of great value. The 100 million acres of rice paddies in the inland delta have great potential for rice cultivation, and irrigated areas near Bamako have potential for growing sugar cane.

Mali has no forests of marketable wood. Except for some minor amounts of gum acacia (used in textile processing) and kapok (used as filling for mattresses), Mali has little potential for forest products in the near future.

Agricultural production in most areas of Mali has changed very little in the past fifty years. The low productivity of the land makes it difficult for the country to increase output. In order to make many necessary improvements, Mali needs agricultural research. Even more important, the nation needs the trained manpower and resources to adapt modern methods to local needs. Better varieties of plants and animals need to be introduced to the farmers in Mali so farmers realize their value and begin to use them.

The Mali government committed a great deal of money to large-scale agricultural development projects in the first years of independence. But it was unable to raise the standard of living for the small farmer. In the long run, the farmers are the ones who will produce much of the surplus necessary to help the country grow.

GROWING INDUSTRY

Like many African countries, Mali has an unemployment problem. Industrialization has seemed to be the answer to this problem, as well as the means of increasing the nation's wealth.

The Chinese have helped build a large textile factory in Ségou to spin the raw cotton that the government hopes to produce. The Chinese have also aided in the construction of a sugar factory for the sugar cane that the government hopes to produce in sufficient quantities. In addition, the Chinese have built a distillery, a cigarette factory, and a match factory. West Germany has contributed a food, oil, and soap factory at Koulikoro; Yugoslavia has donated a cannery in Baguineda and a slaughterhouse and refrigerated meat-storage plant in Gao; North Korea has erected a ceramics factory; the Soviet Union a cement plant; and other countries have contributed other factories.

Some of these factories are perhaps of real value. With cheap labor, the food, oil, and soap factory can probably compete on the world market if there are enough supplies of cottonseed and peanuts. The COMATEX (Malian Textile Company) at Ségou employs a thousand people, but already there is a lack of raw cotton to meet production needs. Current production is not sufficient to justify its cost of 7.5 million dollars. The factory produces twenty-nine-inch-wide cloth that does not sell as well as the fifty-six-inch-wide cloth produced in nearby Ivory Coast.

All of the industrial enterprises are run by the government and are dependent on government-furnished supplies of cotton, peanuts, and other raw materials. This again poses a problem. Without increasing agricultural production, the government finds itself saddled with large debts for plants that run at only partial capacity. These are costs that a relatively poor country cannot easily face.

An even greater obstacle to the country's development, though, is the lack of markets for the goods produced. The ceramic factory at Djikoroni produces expensive items such as cups, plates, flower pots, and ashtrays. But the people of Mali are too poor to afford such luxuries. A few metal trays and bowls and one or two cups are all that an average Malian farm family

Current cotton production in Mali is not as great as the government would like, but cotton is produced in many Malian villages like this one near Ségou.

needs and can afford. The toilet bowls and sinks produced at the factory are also luxuries, since few farmers have running water. Even the rich need only a small quantity of these items, and hotels often import their tableware. As far as foreign competition is concerned, cheaper Japanese and Eastern European goods have the market covered.

The same problems affect the furniture factory and to some extent even the slaughterhouses in Gao and Bamako. The dairy near Bamako, which gathers milk from the low-yield cows in a sixty-mile radius around Bamako, must sell its milk at a cost so high that only the wealthy and a few foreign residents in Bamako can afford it.

Mali's real needs may be best met by regional cooperation and less duplication. There was little need for a cigarette factory in Bamako when Guinea, only six hundred miles away, had one that could not sell half of its potential production. Economic necessity in the rest of the world will provide greater difficulty in getting funds for building such factories. Markets and production are closely tied together, and Mali needs more of both.

TRANSPORTATION

Roads that connect farms to markets are important to further economic development in Mali. There are only 4960 miles of all-weather roads and 870 miles of hard-surfaced roads in the country. Mali has received foreign aid for upkeep and improvement of another 930 miles of road, which will probably include the road to the Ivory Coast; a Saharan route to Gao or Timbuktu is in the planning stage.

Mali's only railroad line is the ancient and outdated metric Dakar-Niger line, with a short extension northeast to Koulikoro on the Niger River. On September 17, 1970, the bridge over the Senegal River at Badougou collapsed while carrying a trainload of people; traffic was cut off for seven months, and many people died. A new bridge and a nine-million-

This vehicle is traveling a secondary Malian road. Because the rains cause much damage, travel is often difficult.

MARK LA POINTE

dollar credit advance by AID and the UN to improve the line promise that this important link with the sea will become even more useful in the years to come.

Air Mali has nine planes, including three DC-3s, one Boeing 727, and five Soviet models. In 1969 Air Mali carried fifty thousand passengers and one thousand metric tons of freight. The airline flies to ten points within the country and to a number of nearby countries. There is a modern international jet airport at Bamako.

COMMUNICATIONS

In Mali, there are two daily papers, *Amin* and *Essor*. *Amin* is published by the National Information Agency, while The Ministry of Information publishes *Essor* ("The Voice of the People"). A monthly magazine called *The Informator* is also published in Mali. A number of other short-term missionary and private publications also appear from time to time.

Radio Mali broadcasts each day throughout the country in French and a number of African languages. Mali's largest transmitter, located on the heights just northeast of Bamako, is fifty kilowatts.

Of the twenty-five hundred telephones in Mali, eighteen hundred are in Bamako. Twenty-nine towns have telephone connections, but only Bamako has dial phones. The government plans to extend dial phones in the next five years to Ségou, Koulikoro, Kati, Mopti, and Kayes.

FUTURE DEVELOPMENT

Mali's further development depends on the country's ability to form cooperative agreements with neighboring countries in order to increase its markets and gain necessary materials. Agricultural production must be increased and less emphasis put on production for production's sake. In the long run, much will depend on Mali's ability to slow population growth as well as to irrigate and grow more food.

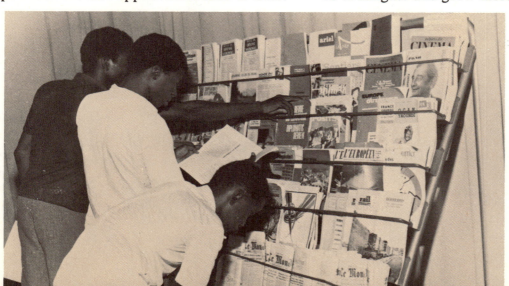

This newspaper and magazine rack in a bookstore in Bamako attracts browsers.

MINISTRY OF INFORMATION

Enchantment of Mali

With its legends, spectacular rock formations, and great rivers, Mali is an interesting and exciting country. Since Mali's independence, many foreigners have discovered the beauty of Mali, and tourism has been on the rise. Many visitors enter Mali via the Dakar-Niger Railroad, which passes through the Kayes region and the Bamako region, stopping at Ségou, Mopti, and the Dogon country, and continuing on to Gao—traveling through the heart of ancient and historic land. A few months are needed to see all the regions, and a lifetime could be spent learning about and understanding all the ethnic groups. But even a rapid tour through the six regions of Mali would give most tourists a general understanding of the country and its people.

REGION OF KAYES

In extreme western Mali is the region of Kayes. This was the first area the French occupied, so there are many historical sites here, as well as natural sites. Fifty miles southeast of Kayes is a spectacular waterfall—Guinea Falls. Rising from the surrounding plains are the Tamboura Cliffs. The ancient French fort at Medina and the fortress of Al-Hajj Umar near Kayes are interesting nineteenth-century historic sites.

Opposite: This spectacular rock formation south of Bamako was created by water and wind erosion.

REGION OF BAMAKO

To the southeast is the region of Bamako. The sights of this region include prehistoric remains in a cave near Kouroukale. Just sixty miles south of Bamako is Kangaba—one of the ancient capitals of the Mali empire. Every seven years, a festival is held at Kangaba, and Mande-speaking peoples gather together from all over Mali, Guinea, and Senegal. Near Kangaba are the Mandinga Mountains. Over these mountains flow streams of white water, occasionally interrupted by rocky outcroppings that form spectacular waterfalls, such as Oyako Falls.

Other sights of interest include Klassajou Dam, with its many egrets, and Baoulé National Park, along the Baoulé River. The most interesting sight in the region, however, is the capital, Bamako. With a population of 250,000, this savanna city stretches along the majestic Niger River for about six miles. As Mali's largest city, Bamako is a symbol of modern Mali; yet at the same time, it reflects many of the old ways.

Bamako was a village of about four hundred people when the French colonel,

Washday on the shores of the Senegal River in the region of Kayes.

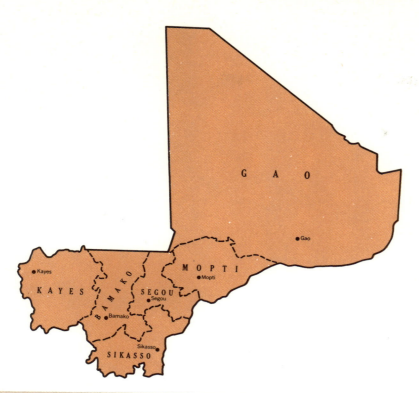

Left: The six regions of Mali. Below: A pirogue on the Senegal River in the region of Kayes. Pirogues are a common means of travel on the rivers of Mali.

Borgnis-Desbordes, arrived in 1883. In 1903 the city became the capital of the French Sudan. Two years later, the railroad connected Bamako with Dakar (in Senegal).

Today Bamako has a number of good hotels, including the moderately priced Majestic, which serves excellent African and European meals. A few miles outside of Bamako is a beautiful, tree-shaded hotel called Lido, with lush gardens and a fine restaurant. The government-owned Grand Hotel in downtown Bamako has a rather expensive restaurant. The new 17-story, 170-room Hotel d'Amite is the most deluxe hotel in the country. There are 30 apartments, a nightclub, two large restaurants, and beauty shops; also included in the hotel complex are a snack bar, a post office, African and European boutiques, a bank, a large theater, and two swimming pools.

The Koulouba Heights outside the city offer a panoramic view of Bamako. The new sports stadium, the central mosque, and the Roman Catholic cathedral all stand out against the rest of the city. Also on the Heights are the presidential palace and the old colonial offices.

Excellent wood carvings are sold in shops throughout the city, often at reasonable prices. The Bamako market, in the center of the city, has imitation Sudanese architecture; its color and animation make it an interesting market. It is easy to fall into the lively spirit of the market, bargaining furiously for a handwoven Bambara blanket or a handmade basket.

The artists' market is located across the square from the central mosque. Here beautiful filigree, aluminum, silver, and gold work can be purchased from craftsmen, as well as hand-worked sandals, bags, and other leather goods, and ivory and wood carvings. Facing the square is the National Arts Institute, which houses authentic masterpieces.

REGION OF SIKASSO

In the extreme southern tip of the country is the region of Sikasso. South of Bamako, the blacktop road passes through Oulessebougou, with its rice fields and Roman Catholic mission church. Almost halfway to Sikasso is the town of Bougouni, with forty-five hundred people. The administrative center of a heavily forested area, Bougouni produces oranges, pineapples, and bananas, as well as rice and peanuts. In some streams west of the town, gold is still panned in the traditional manner. Throughout this area are underground caves once used as tombs. The caves are respected by the local people,

The capital city of Bamako is Mali's largest city. The modern sports stadium is one of the city's main attractions. Opposite top: The theater at Omnisport Stadium. Opposite bottom: Omnisport Stadium.

who do not explore or visit them. From Bougouni, the road turns east to Sikasso and on to Upper Volta, passing antelope, wild boars, and birds.

At Sikasso is a great mound that was built as a rest area and observation point for the nineteenth-century King Tieba. This town of seventeen thousand people is the center of an area historically important for its resistance against both the Malinke and the French. At Sikasso are a number of ruins and moats that were built for defense in the nineteenth century. Local men delight in telling visitors the history of the area.

REGION OF SÉGOU

Directly north is Ségou, the capital of Mali's most populous region. In the heart of Bambara country, Ségou is perhaps the ethnic center as well as the geographical center of the country. This city stretches four miles along the Niger River about 150 miles northeast of Bamako. Once the capital of the Bambara empire and the empire of Al-Hajj Umar, Ségou was lost to French occupation in 1890. It became the center of a huge irrigation project in the 1940s.

The Markala Dam on the Niger River, region of Ségou (below),
is one of the longest dams in the world built exclusively for irrigation.
Opposite: The main marketplace in Ségou.

Above: The Mopti market has Sudanese "canaris" for sale. They are used to carry water. Below: The Mopti fish market is the greatest fish market in West Africa. More than thirteen thousand tons of dried and smoked fish are exported each year.

A seven-mile drive along this dike leads to Mopti, the "Venice of Mali."

Near Ségou is a planned marketing and industrial complex at Markala. In the region of Ségou are also Tenenkou (the ancient capital of Macina) and Dia (one of the oldest towns in the nation).

REGION OF MOPTI

To the northeast, the road follows the Niger River to Mopti, the second-most-important commercial city in Mali. In Mopti, where the Niger River joins the Bani River, is the greatest fish market in West Africa. Each day tons of dry, smoked, and fresh fish are sent to markets throughout Mali and surrounding countries.

Located on three islands and connected by dikes, Mopti has been called the "Venice of Mali." Getting to Mopti requires a seven-mile drive along a dike. In Mopti's market, rice, onions, cattle, woven Massa blankets, and fish are sold, as well as local embroidery and pottery.

Nearly eighty miles south is Jenne, an ancient political, trade, and religious city that still holds an important place in the widespread networks of Islamic teaching throughout West Africa. Once Jenne was a rival of Timbuktu.

Located on the great flood plain of the Bani River, Jenne is surrounded by water much of the year. It has served as a safe storage place for trade goods since its founding over a thousand years ago. Jenne's streets are very broad; its houses, a blend of North African and local styles, have been rebuilt again and again since the fourteenth century.

The great mosque of Jenne has a hundred huge pillars. The mosque is on a large, open square in this walled city. At its feet, Muslim scholars still study the fine points of Islamic law, as they have done for several hundred years.

Above: Mopti Harbor, at the confluence of the Niger and Bani rivers. Below: The village of Sofara in the region of Mopti. The typically Sudanese architecture uses "banco" (dirt bricks) as the main construction material. Opposite: The Mopti mosque.

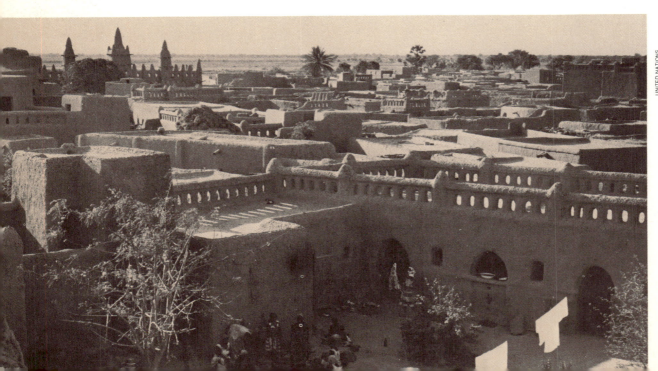

Left: This mother stands with her child in front of their banco home in the village of Sofara. Opposite: Dogon cliff dwellings in the Bandiagara Cliffs in the region of Mopti.

On the edge of the great Bandiagara Cliffs east of Mopti, one can see far across the great plains of West Africa to the Sahara in the northeast. Six Dogon villages stretch side by side across the face of the cliff. The Dogon people and their cliff dwellings are unique in Mali. Perhaps the most conservative and interesting people in the nation, the Dogon are a farming and hunting people, who carry on a constant struggle against a hostile environment. With their traditional indigo-dyed hand-woven clothes, the Dogon live in stone and mud houses perched on or near the cliffs.

For a token fee, a young Dogon guide will loan a visitor a local straw hat against the blazing sun and guide him down the cliff to Irely and the other villages. The Dogon use closed caves in the cliffs as granaries, as safe storage places for their dance masks and other ceremonial items, and as burial grounds for their dead.

On these cliffs, water is the all-precious gift of the gods—in fact, the concept of God to a Dogon means water. The Dogon god dies, is resurrected, and comes back to earth in the form of rain. The world-famous Dogon sculpture in masks, iron, and granary doors can help explain the mysteries of Dogon religion. Both Dogon art and Dogon ceremonial dances tell the story of the cliffs, the water that is stored there, and the Dogon ancestors' gradual movement south from the Sahara.

The Malian Company of Navigation offers first-class riverboat accommodations for part of the year from Mopti to Gao. Gliding along the river in a boat on this four-day trip, Tuareg camps can often be

The Dogon are perhaps the most interesting people in Mali. A hunting and farming people, they live in unique cliff dwellings east of Mopti. Opposite: This Dogon man spreads balls of chopped, soaked onions out to dry. The Dogon market these onion balls throughout Mali. Right: Dogon dancers do the traditional Dance of the Mask. Below: Prehistoric Dogon cave paintings help link present-day Dogon people with their past.

seen, as well as Bozo fishermen on the riverbank or huge flocks of sheep and goats being led down to the water's edge.

REGION OF GAO

Along the Niger River on the way to Gao is the fabled and mysterious Timbuktu. This "Key to the Sahara" or "Queen of the Desert," as the city has been called, serves as headquarters of the vast region of Gao. This region is larger than the state of Oregon, but it has fewer than one thousand people. The region of Gao, which stretches north to Algeria, is the home of Moors and Tuareg, and it produces little but livestock and salt.

Lonely and beautiful, the city of Timbuktu is located near ancient wells. This historical city dates back at least as far as the eleventh century, when it was a famous Islamic center of learning. Once an important caravan terminal, Timbuktu became important because salt that was mined in the Sahara could be loaded on boats to travel the Niger River; goods from the south came by boat and were loaded on camels at Timbuktu. Salt caravans with thousands of camels still arrive in Timbuktu annually; the camels are loaded with great chunks of salt cut in the mines of Taoudeni in the central Sahara.

The city of Gao, southeast of Timbuktu, is the ancient capital of the Songhai Empire. The buildings in this beautiful city look like those of a North African town. Gao is still an important starting point for trans-Saharan travelers, as well as a market town for a large area in Mali, Upper Volta, and Niger. Nearby are the ruins of Songhai mosques and tombs of past emperors.

TOURISM

Because Mali is not a rich, industrial nation, traveling in the country is made difficult by delays, transportation difficulties, and sometimes communication breakdowns. But Mali offers rich experiences in a world of myth, story, song, dance, art, and history. For Mali, tourism is a future hope. The income from the tourist industry is one of a very few ways by which the nation could gain enough money to help it break free of its present economic binds. Perhaps the glories of the past can be made to yield direct benefits to Mali's present and future generations.

Opposite: The ancient desert city of Timbuktu in the region of Gao dates back at least as far as the eleventh century, when it was a famous Islamic center of learning.

Handy Reference Section

Political:

Official Name—Republic of Mali
Capital—Bamako
Monetary Unit—Malian Franc (430 francs = US $1)
Official Language—French
Independence Day—September 22, 1960
Flag—Three vertical bands (from left to right): green, yellow, and red
National Motto—"One people, one goal, one faith"
National Symbol—Stylized dove, flying to the left over an equally stylized "Sudanese" mosque or palace. To the lower left and right of the mosque are drawn bows with arrows pointed out-ward, as if in defense. At the bottom, in a rising sun and surrounding the whole, are the words "Republic of Mali: One People, One Goal, One Faith."

Geographical:

Area—465,000 square miles
Highest Point—2624 feet, near Bandiagara
Greatest Width (southwest to northeast)—1180 miles
Greatest Length (north to south)—1045 miles
Narrowest Length (north to south)—180 miles

POPULATION

Population (1969 estimate)—4,900,000
Population Density—less than ten persons per square mile
Population Growth Rate—2.5 percent
Births (per 1000)—47.5
Life Expectancy—50 percent of population under twenty, only 5 percent over sixty years of age
Infant Mortality (per 1000)—120

Ethnic Groups:

Mande (Bambara, Malinke)	50 percent
Fulbé	17 percent
Voltaic groups	12 percent
Songhai	6 percent
Tuareg and Moors	9 percent
Others	6 percent

PRINCIPAL CITIES

Bamako	200,000
Mopti	32,000
Ségou	27,000
Kayes	24,000
Sikasso	17,000
Gao	15,000
Timbuktu	14,000

REGIONS

Kayes
Bamako
Sikasso
Ségou
Mopti
Gao

NATIONAL DAYS

January 1—New Year's Day
January 20—Armed Forces Day
May 1—Labor Day
May 25—Africa Day
September 22—Independence Day
December 25—Christmas Day
Days not fixed—Easter, Muhammad's Birthday, End of Ramadan (Muslim month of fasting)

SELECTED BAMBARA VOCABULARY

deme	to help
terikeh	friend
wari	money
minan	baggage
bi	today
mako	need
i ni sogoma	good morning
wulu	dog
dono koro	rooster
sini	tomorrow
dji	water
mosso	woman
tubabu	European
bele bele	big
djeli keh	praise singer
keh	man
nono	milk
kili	egg
kuma	to speak
kolon	well
malo	rice
sogo	meat
djon	who?

60,000 B.C.—Hunters lived in northern Mali

40,000 B.C.—Hunters with fire lived in southern Mali

7000 B.C.—Sahara begins to become drier

4000 B.C.—Farmers lived in Mali

700-1076 A.D.—Ghana empire flourishes

1204-1550—Mali empire flourishes

1231—Battle of Kirina

1325—Fall of Gao to Mali

1464-1591—Songhai empire flourishes

1740-1819—Bambara kingdoms flourish

1819-1862—Macina empire flourishes

1848-1893—Tokolor empire flourishes

1852-1898—Samori's empire flourishes

1855—French establish Fort Medina

1895—French government established at Kayes

1904—Railroad reaches Bamako

1944—Brazzaville Conference meets

1946—RDA established

1956—Equal voting rights granted to black citizens of French colonies

1957—Sudanese Union Party controls National Assembly

1958—Mali votes to remain with French Union

1959—Mali joins Senegal in Mali Federation (April)

1960—Independence declared; Senegal and Mali become separate nations

1962—Creation of an independent currency for Mali

1967—Currency devalued 50 percent

1968—President Keita deposed; drought begins (November)

1969—Moussa Traoré becomes acting president (September)

1973—Aid sent to relieve disaster from drought

Index

Italicized page numbers indicate illustrations.

About the Authors

Already the author of seventy-three books published by Childrens Press, **Allan Carpenter** is on his way again with the forty-two book "Enchantment of Africa" series. Except for a few years spent founding, editing, and publishing a teachers' magazine, Allan has worked as a free-lance writer of books and magazine articles. During his many years in publishing, he has perfected a highly organized approach to handling large volumes of material—after extensive traveling and having collected all possible materials, he systematically reviews and organizes everything. From his apartment high in the magnificent John Hancock Building, Allan recalls: "My collection and assimilation of materials on the states and countries began before the publication of my first book when I was twenty years old." When not writing or traveling, Allan also enjoys music—he has been the principal string bass player for the Chicago Business Men's Orchestra for twenty-five years.

Co-author **Tom O'Toole** has written and lectured widely on African studies since returning in 1965 from Peace Corps service in Guinea, West Africa. He wrote the article on Guinea in the 1974 *Encyclopaedia Britannica*. With Dan Schafer of the University of North Florida he has produced a series of eight films on West African Peoples and Cultures. He was instructor of African History at the General College of the University of Minnesota for four years. He taught African History and Culture at Western Carolina University for two years. Currently he is a Research Associate in the Social Studies Curriculum Center, Carnegie-Mellon University, where he is developing a self-paced program of instruction in African History under the direction of Dr. Barry K. Beyer. In his leisure time, Tom enjoys camping and gardening. Both he and his wife, Ann, are involved in a community education effort to inform people about the world food crisis.

Co-author **Mark D. LaPointe**, born in Maine in 1941, spent seven years in West Africa. From 1963 to 1965 he served with the Peace Corps in Guinea. After training at the National Center for Disease Control in Atlanta, Georgia, he was assigned as Operations Officer of the U.S. Public Health Service/World Health Organization's Smallpox-Measles Eradication Program in Gabon and Mali from 1966 to 1971. He worked as a Public Health Advisor to the New Orleans Bureau of Tuberculosis Control and is currently Tuberculosis Advisor for the central Pennsylvania area. In early 1975 he was granted a leave of absence to join the World Health Organization's Smallpox Eradication Program in Bangladesh.